GREAT GIFTS™

GREET THE SEASON

Copyright © 1996 Cy DeCosse Incorporated 5900 Green Oak Drive Minnetonka, Minnesota 55343
1-800-328-3895 All rights reserved Printed in U.S.A.

Library of Congress Cataloging-in-Publication Data Greet the season. p. cm. — Includes index. ISBN 0-86573-987-0 —
1. Holiday decorations. 2. Handicraft. 3. Gifts. I. Cy DeCosse Incorporated.   TT900.H6G74 1996
745.594'1 — dc20 96-10563 CIP

Table of Contents

GIFTS
for the Bath

Bathroom accessories and special bath items designed to pamper can be thoughtful gifts at holiday time. Overnight guests will appreciate boxes of bath items packaged just for them, and when you go visiting, you can give your hosts something to enhance their home or indulge themselves.

All kinds of specialized bath items, including soaps, oils, towels, sponges, and bath salts, are available at bath and home stores. Purchase a decorative glass bowl and fill it with assorted bath beads; many beads are available in holiday shapes and colors. Nestle a bottle of scented bath oil, lotion, or soap in the middle of the beads, and embellish the bowl with holiday berries and greenery.

For young visitors to your home, personalize a large, colorful plastic bucket; then fill it with fun soaps, baby shampoo, and bath toys. Invite children to take everything with them when they go home.

A whimsical gift for young and old alike is a bubble-gum machine filled with colorful bath beads. Hang a bag of pennies on the machine to get them started.

DECORATIVE
Candles

Candles create a warm, inviting glow in any room of the house, and candle holder and candle combinations are popular, widely accepted gifts. Pillar candles can be embellished with decorative nail heads and ribbon. Enhance simple taper candles with interesting presentations, using latex fruit, glass chimneys, or embellished terra-cotta pots as candle holders. Accent small floating candles; then combine them with a shallow bowl and glass stones for setting them off.

A favorite style of decorative candle is the rolled beeswax candle, but they can be expensive when purchased at a specialty store. Sheets of honeycomb beeswax are available for a fraction of the cost at craft stores and mail-order suppliers. Make your own in a variety of styles, shown on pages 10 and 11.

Pillar Candles

🎁

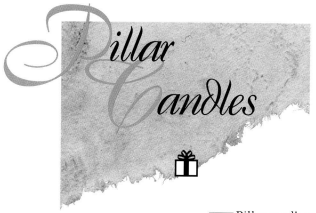

1 Pillar candles can be quickly embellished with decorative nail heads. To avoid excessive cracking, use nail heads with prongs not longer than 1/8" (3 mm) and press the prongs gently into candles. Further accent these candles with French ribbons. Combine assorted sizes and styles of candles, so a clustered display can be created.

Floating Candles

🎁

☞ *Combine several candles with a clear, heavy dish; include smooth, colored-glass stones for placement over bottom of dish.*

1 Cover the wicks of floating candles with transparent tape. Spray tops of candles with aerosol adhesive; sprinkle with fine or ultrafine glitter. Remove tape.

☞ *Cut holes in latex fruit to accommodate candles; spray the fruit with silver or gold metallic aerosol acrylic paint. Allow to dry. Insert silver or gold taper candles in prepared fruit.*

☞ *Glass chimneys can be surrounded by sprigs of holly and evergreen or twigs. Secure embellishments to chimneys with floral adhesive or rubber bands, which are then concealed with ribbon or raffia.*

☞ *Paint terra-cotta flowerpots with aerosol acrylic paint in metallic or holiday colors. Embellish pots with ribbon or greenery. Fill pots with floral foam to hold candles, and randomly insert taper candles into foam; conceal foam with sprigs of greenery.*

Beeswax Taper Candles

MATERIALS

❖Beeswax sheets, 8½" × 16¾" (21.8 × 42.4 cm)
❖2/0 candle wicking ❖Rotary cutter, such as a
pizza cutter, or sharp knife ❖Ruler

Basic Tapers

Makes two 8" × ½" (20.5 × 1.3 cm) candles

1 Cut one beeswax sheet in half crosswise. Make an angled cut across upper long end of one half, from the corner at one side to a point ¾" (2 cm) from corner on opposite side. Cut the wick to two 9" (23 cm) lengths; place wicks on the longest edge of each sheet.

2 Roll edge of sheet tightly and evenly over wick; press firmly, embedding wick in beeswax. Roll sheet, keeping even pressure along length of candle; keep lower edge even. Seal outer edge of sheet to outside of candle by pressing firmly along edge.

Spiral Tapers

Makes two 16" (40.5 cm) candles

1 Cut one beeswax sheet in half diagonally. Cut wick to two 17" (43 cm) lengths; place wicks on long straight edge of each triangle.

2 Roll candles as in step 2, opposite, keeping lower edges even. Seal outer edge of sheets to outside of the candle by pressing firmly along the edge at base.

☞ *For fluted tapers, flare diagonal edges of rolled candles by holding the beeswax between the thumb and forefinger and pulling out gently.*

Two-color Spiral Tapers

Makes two 16" (40.5 cm) candles

1 Cut two different-colored sheets of beeswax and two wicks as in step 1, above. Set aside one triangle of each color. Cut 1" (2.5 cm) from lower edge of one triangle.

2 Place shorter triangle on table; place taller triangle of second color on top, aligning lower edges. Place wick on long straight edge of layered triangles. Roll candle as in step 2, above. Repeat with remaining triangles and wick.

☞ *Flute edges, if desired, as described above.*

Pinecone kindler BASKET

What could be better than a relaxing evening in front of the fire? For an inexpensive gift that is both useful and decorative, create a fire-starter basket filled with pinecone kindlers. If desired, add color sticks and long fireplace matches.

Pinecones dipped in paraffin wax burn hot for about 20 minutes while your fire gets started. They can be colored red and scented with cinnamon, or colored green and scented with pine, if desired. Most of the materials you'll need can be found in craft stores. To light a fire, center a pinecone kindler under stacked firewood and light its wick.

Pinecone Kindlers

MATERIALS

❖Double boiler ❖Paraffin wax, approximately 1 lb. (450 g) per six pinecones ❖Candle color squares and candle scent squares, one square each per 1 lb. (450 g) of wax ❖Candy thermometer ❖Muffin cups ❖Nonstick vegetable cooking spray ❖Wax-coated candlewicks, 6" (15 cm) lengths ❖Pinecones, 2" (5 cm) diameter ❖Tongs

1 Melt 1 lb. (450 g) paraffin wax in top of double boiler over boiling water. Add one square each of candle color and candle scent. Mix gently, using wooden spoon.

2 Spray muffin cups with nonstick cooking spray. Place one end of candlewicks in each muffin cup; allow other end to hang over sides of cups.

3 Cool melted paraffin to about 160°F (70°C). Dip pinecone in paraffin, turning to coat; remove with tongs and place coated pinecone upright in muffin cup. Repeat with remaining pinecones.

14

4 Remove top of double boiler containing remaining wax; dry outside of pan to prevent water from dripping onto pinecones. Slowly pour ½" (1.3 cm) melted wax into each muffin cup at base of pinecone.

5 Allow kindlers to cool completely. Remove from muffin cups. Arrange in gift basket with note card giving instructions for use.

☞ *For easier cleanup, line muffin cups with foil before spraying and adding pinecones.*

☞ *Use old or inexpensive utensils for making pinecone kindlers.*

HOLIDAY
Baker's aprons

Delight the bakers on your gift list with a special apron and all the tools necessary to turn out their own holiday cutout cookies. Purchase an apron in holiday colors or the recipient's favorite color; then personalize it with fabric paints, embroidery, cross-stitch, small buttons, ribbons, or beads.

Roll a rolling pin and wooden spoon inside the apron, and tie it up, using the apron ties. Attach cookie cutters and measuring spoons to the ends with ribbons or raffia. You could even tuck a small cookie book under the apron ties, include a gift certificate to a cookware store, or attach a subscription to a favorite food magazine.

A Gift For You

Decoupage
HOLIDAY PLATES

A favorite gift for holiday time is a plateful of homemade goodies. Add to this special gift by presenting your treats on a decorative plate that will be used for years to come.

You can transform an inexpensive clear glass plate by using simple decoupage techniques and motifs cut from high-quality wrapping paper or greeting cards. Motifs are secured to the back of the plate with decoupage medium. For a background with a dimensional effect, paints are applied with a sponging technique. Finally, aerosol acrylic sealer is used as a sealer over the paint.

Decoupage Plates

MATERIALS

❖Clear glass plate ❖High-quality wrapping paper with desired motifs ❖Scissors with fine, sharp blades and points ❖Decoupage medium; brush or sponge applicator ❖Sponge or brayer ❖Acrylic paints; small piece of natural sea sponge, for applying paints ❖Aerosol acrylic paint, optional ❖Aerosol clear acrylic sealer

1 Cut desired motifs from wrapping paper. Cut any intricate motifs from paper by first cutting a smooth curve around design. Cut details by holding scissors stationary and moving motif.

2 Trace the plate on piece of paper; plan placement of motifs. Clean back of plate thoroughly, using glass cleaner and lint-free rag; place plate facedown on table.

3 Apply a thin layer of decoupage medium to front of foreground motif, using sponge applicator, brush, or finger. Position motif on back of plate; smooth out with dampened sponge or brayer. (Any excess decoupage medium around edges of motif will not show when plate is painted.)

4 Continue applying motifs as desired, working from foreground to background if motifs are layered. Allow to dry. Apply thin coat of decoupage medium to back of motifs as a sealer; allow to dry.

5 Apply lightest color of acrylic paint to back of plate, using sea sponge; apply sparingly. Allow to dry. Apply the remaining layers of paint, finishing with the darkest color. If desired, paint back of plate a solid color, using aerosol acrylic paint. Allow to dry.

6 Personalize plate on back with your signature and the date, using permanent-ink marking pen. Mark where signature won't show through front of plate, if back of plate is not painted a solid color. Apply light coat of aerosol acrylic sealer; allow to dry. Apply second coat.

☞ *If heavy paper, such as a greeting card, is used, reduce the thickness by peeling away one or more layers of paper.*

☞ *Use curved cuticle scissors to cut out intricate, curved motifs. Cut with points of blades away from motif.*

PHOTO
Memory boxes

Photographs are a favorite way to reminisce about good times and holiday events. Give a complete photo memory box to your friends and family, and they'll remember your thoughtfulness every time they pull it out.

Purchase ready-made photograph and negative storage box sets, or make your own by embellishing sturdy boxes and filling them with notecards, divider tabs, and plastic photo negative sleeves. Include a single-use camera, film, coupons for film development, a decorative frame, or a small photo album. See *Memory Books* on page 24 for ideas on how to personalize photo albums.

Memory books

Create one-of-a-kind photo albums, journals, and address books by covering them with decorative paper or fabric. Embellish the front of the book with tassels, bows, small framed photos, buttons, fabric or paper collages, or simple mementos. Choose the embellishments to suit your recipient.

You can present your customized book with empty pages, so the recipient can have the fun of filling them. For example, if the book is for a traveler, you could wrap it with a map, embellish it with a compass, and tell your friend to use the book as a journal for documenting his next trip. Or, fill a small photo album with favorite pictures and add captions. Produce a family history for your parents, all the way from their wedding day to today.

Paper-covered Memory book

MATERIALS

❖Blank book or photo album ❖Art paper or wrapping paper, in two coordinating colors or patterns ❖Aerosol adhesive ❖Desired embellishments

1 Cut the paper 1" (2.5 cm) larger than the opened book on all sides. Place the paper facedown on work surface. Apply a generous coat of aerosol adhesive to the back of paper.

2 Place spine of book in center of paper; press gently. Working from spine to edge of cover, smooth one side of paper over front cover of book; rub paper into groove along spine with end of pencil. Repeat for back of book.

3 Fold excess paper from sides of front and back covers to inside of book; press and smooth paper to the inside of covers. Cut notches in paper along top and bottom of book at the spine. Fold paper in at spine.

4 Fold excess paper from tops and bottoms of the cover to inside of book; fold in corners as you would when wrapping a gift. Press and smooth the paper to inside of cover.

5 Cut second paper into two sheets with dimensions 1/4" (6 mm) smaller than inside of covers on all sides. Spray backs of sheets with aerosol adhesive. Press sheets to inside of front and back covers. Embellish book as desired.

☞ Use this same method to make a fabric cover. Lightweight fabric works best.

☞ Tie ribbon or raffia around length of inside of front cover and spine for embellishment.

PERSONALIZED *Calendars*

A personalized calendar is perfect for that busy person on your gift list who appreciates reminders for birthdays, anniversaries, or family events. Select wall calendars for home use and appointment books for the office.

Record all important dates. For birthdays and anniversaries, remember to include the year, such as the person's age or which wedding anniversary it is. You can even include fun facts, such as vacation dates, family reunions, the dog's birthday, or the day someone in the family won a small lottery.

Make your marked dates stand out by using colored markers, stickers, stamps, or small drawings. You could glue sequins and small streamers on New Year's Eve or small photos on dates for birthdays.

a

b

c

Bottled gifts

Glass bottles and decanters are available in a wide variety of shapes, styles, and colors. When they are embellished with ribbons, dried naturals, or decorative bottle stoppers, they make easy and inexpensive gifts. Go a step further and fill them with herbal cooking oils or vinegars, homemade vanilla, scented bath oils, or bath salts. Give individual bottles, or select complementary bottles for a collection.

Bottled gifts include:

a) Herb-flavored vinegar, *b)* flavored cooking oil, *c)* bath salts, *d)* scented bath oil, *e)* homemade vanilla extract.

Stone bottle Stopper

MATERIALS

❖Rough-edged stone or crystal ❖Bottle cork
❖Instant-bond glue ❖Thin, flexible copper wire
❖Needlenose pliers

1 Attach stone or crystal to top of cork, using instant-bond glue; hold until set.

2 Wrap the wire around stone and top of the cork several times, crisscrossing wire several times over stone.

3 Twist end of wire around crisscrossed wire to secure, using pliers.

☞ *Select a stone in an appropriate size for the cork and bottle on which it will go.*

Flavored cooking Oils

1 Wash and dry fresh herbs, such as rosemary, tarragon, thyme, basil, or dill; place about three sprigs of selected herb in bottle. Fill bottle with olive oil or canola oil; cap tightly. Store in refrigerator for three weeks before using, shaking bottle occasionally to distribute flavor.

☞ *Dried chili peppers can also be used with this technique to make flavored oil.*

☞ *Advise gift recipients to keep oil refrigerated and to use it within one month of having received it.*

1 Wash and dry fresh herbs, such as those mentioned in *Flavored Cooking Oils*; place two or three sprigs of selected herb in bottle. Fill bottle with white wine vinegar or cider vinegar; cap tightly. Place bottle in sunny place for two to three weeks. Strain vinegar; return vinegar to clean bottle. Store in cool, dark place.

☞ *To speed up process, heat vinegar before filling bottle.*

☞ *Add more fresh herbs to bottle after vinegar has been strained.*

1 Place undyed dried flowers in decorative bottle, if desired. In a measuring cup, combine 100% pure sesame oil and pure scented essential oil; use 1/2 cup (125 mL) sesame oil to 2 teaspoons (10 mL) essential oil. Fill bottle with prepared oil. Use bath oil sparingly in bath water or for body massages.

1 Split a vanilla bean, lengthwise; place in small, decorative bottle. Fill bottle with quality vodka; use 3/4 cup (175 mL) vodka to one bean. Cap bottle tightly. For maximum flavor, let extract steep for several months. Store in cool, dark place.

☞ *Vanilla beans are available in many supermarkets.*

☞ *After extract is used up, vanilla bean can be air-dried, then buried in granulated sugar, for flavored sugar.*

Wine & Champagne GIFTS

A bottle of wine or champagne is the quintessential gift to take when you go visiting. But just because wine is a simple gift doesn't mean its presentation has to be typical.

Arrange small bottles of assorted wines in a sleigh-shaped basket embellished with garland and festive ribbon. Fill a wine bucket with reusable plastic ice cubes shaped like stars, a bottle of champagne, and two champagne flutes. Purchase a set of large wine glasses, decorate them with ribbon and tissue, and place a small bottle of wine in each glass.

Wine accessories, such as a corkscrew, foil cutter, decorative bottle stoppers, or a drip catcher, can be included in a small pouch attached to the neck of the bottle. Or hang small ornaments around the neck of the bottle and embellish them with ribbon or greenery.

GIFT Certificates

Gift certificates are the perfect gift for that hard-to-shop-for person on your list. They save you the frustration of trying to guess what that person needs or wants, and your gift recipient will have the fun of buying something he or she doesn't have to actually pay for.

Create a special card to hold your gift certificate. If the certificate is from a clothing store, make a card in the shape of a shirt. Gifts for dad can be disguised in a card shaped like a tie which is presented in a tie box. Get him a gift certificate at a favorite restaurant or a local golf-supply shop.

For customized gift giving, make your own gift certificates, or even mock charge cards. A personalized charge card can be used for dinner and a movie, a night of baby-sitting, a car wash, or whatever you wish. Include a list of potential uses with the card.

Certificate

DAD*S
34 605 412

Gift certificate Card

MATERIALS

❖Heavy, printed paper ❖Scrap paper for making pattern ❖Transparent tape or masking tape

🎁

☞ *Select patterned paper that suits the design you've chosen. For example, paper with stripes or a small pattern is appropriate for a necktie-shaped card.*

☞ *Embellish front of card as desired. A gold button acts as a tie pin, or regular buttons embellish a shirt front.*

1 Draw desired design on scrap paper to make pattern. Cut pattern from paper. Cut printed paper to twice the length of pattern; fold printed paper in half crosswise.

2 Position the pattern on the folded paper so that the top of pattern is along fold. Secure the pattern to folded paper with tape. Cut the folded paper along pattern edges through tape; do not cut folded side.

3 Cut small diagonal slits in back flap of card where corners of certificate will go. Insert corners of certificate in slits to secure. Write message inside card. Place card in gift box, and wrap.

1 Trace a real credit card shape onto mat board, using pencil. Cut out shape with mat knife; round corners of card with craft scissors, if necessary.

2 Place rub-on transfers on card in desired position for lettering, numbers, and embellishments. If desired, secure paper cutouts to card, using paper cement.

Mock charge Card

MATERIALS

❖Mat board ❖Mat knife ❖Rub-on transfers
❖Paper cutouts, optional
❖Paper cement, optional

3 Present card in an envelope with instructions on how it may be used.

☞ *If desired, handwrite information directly on card, using permanent-ink marker.*

☞ *Use charge card as a gift tag on packages, or slip it inside a greeting card.*

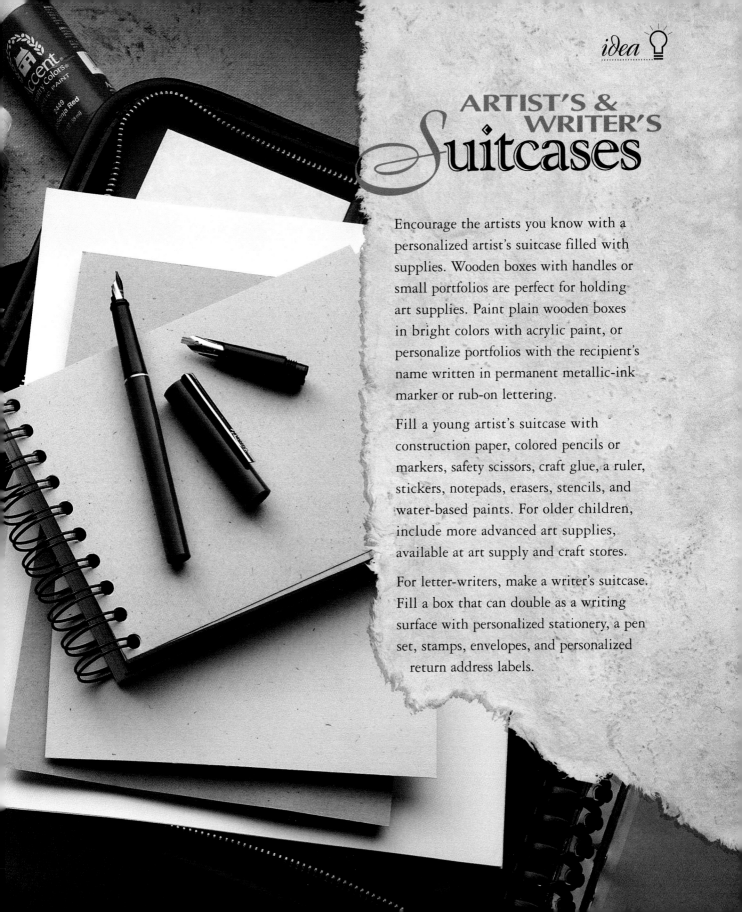

ARTIST'S & WRITER'S Suitcases

Encourage the artists you know with a personalized artist's suitcase filled with supplies. Wooden boxes with handles or small portfolios are perfect for holding art supplies. Paint plain wooden boxes in bright colors with acrylic paint, or personalize portfolios with the recipient's name written in permanent metallic-ink marker or rub-on lettering.

Fill a young artist's suitcase with construction paper, colored pencils or markers, safety scissors, craft glue, a ruler, stickers, notepads, erasers, stencils, and water-based paints. For older children, include more advanced art supplies, available at art supply and craft stores.

For letter-writers, make a writer's suitcase. Fill a box that can double as a writing surface with personalized stationery, a pen set, stamps, envelopes, and personalized return address labels.

DECORATIVE
Bird feeders

Luring our feathered friends to feed outside our windows adds to the homey feeling of the holidays. Help others enjoy the birds by giving them decorative bird feeders. Purchase bell-shaped seed treats or fill bird feeders with sunflower seeds. Decorate them with greenery and other nontoxic embellishments.

Decorate a small pine tree with a variety of bird-treat ornaments. Cover pinecones with peanut butter and roll them in a birdseed mix; attach a loop of raffia for a hanger. String popcorn for a garland. Make orange baskets by cutting oranges in half, hollowing out the peels, tying raffia handles on them, and filling them with birdseed and raisins. Tie fresh orange slices on tree branches, too.

Place this small tree in a large basket so it can be enjoyed on a patio or apartment balcony.

FABULOUS *Food* presentations

Plates of holiday goodies are the quintessential holiday gift. Whether you are giving home-baked cookies or specially purchased holiday candies, or are taking a salad to a party, you can enhance your gift through its presentation.

Line sleigh- or star-shaped baskets with foil or plastic wrap, and fill them with cookies or bars. Embellish the baskets with holiday greenery and ribbons. Make pouches for cookies or candies by placing them in the center of a large circle of netting; gather the netting at the top, and secure with ribbon.

Deli salads in their containers can be slipped inside reproduction vintage tins and served directly from the tin. Line holiday baskets with several layers of plastic wrap or a washed plastic plant liner, and spoon the salad into the lined basket. Or garnish a salad platter with assorted greens and herbs.

Embellished food Basket

MATERIALS

❖Basket with open weave ❖Artificial pine garland ❖Mylar® star garland ❖Sleigh bells ❖22-gauge brass wire ❖Plastic wrap or foil

1 Cut sprigs from garland. Wind through open weave of basket. Wind star garland along pine garland as an accent.

2 Secure sleigh bells randomly along garland and basket handle, using brass wire. Line basket with plastic wrap or foil; fill basket with cookies, candies, bars, or mixed nuts.

☞ *Use colored plastic wrap to line basket.*

Salad Platter

MATERIALS

❖Platter ❖Salad ❖Fresh herbs ❖Fresh greens, such as arugula or watercress ❖Fresh or dried citrus slices, such as orange, lemon, or lime

1 Mound salad in center of platter. Arrange ring of herbs, fresh greens, and citrus slices around the salad. Garnish center of salad with sprigs of fresh herbs or greens.

☞ *Cover platter with plastic wrap to transport it.*

Candy Tree

MATERIALS

❖Styrofoam® cone in desired size ❖Foil wrapping paper ❖Transparent tape ❖Assorted wrapped candies ❖Decorative cocktail toothpicks or floral pins

1 Wrap cone with foil wrapping paper; secure with transparent tape.

2 Secure candies to the cone, using toothpicks or floral pins. Begin at the bottom of the cone; alternate colors, and overlap the candies slightly.

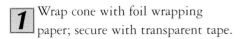

☞ *Fill large coffee mug with coffee-flavored candies and candied espresso beans.*

☞ *Fill a glass beer mug with root beer barrel candies or chocolate-dipped pretzels that have been wrapped in colored plastic wrap.*

CREATIVE
Bread baskets

Nothing evokes warm feelings of home and comfort better than bread—be it a freshly baked banana bread cooling on your countertop or crusty, European-style loaves from the bakery. With the advent of bread machines and specialty bakeries, our love affair with bread has been intensified.

Bakeries offer a wide variety of specialty breads, and they almost always guarantee a fresh, delicious product. To showcase fresh bread, purchase a basket and fill it with your favorite bread. Add to the gift by including a bread knife, bread board, and terra-cotta bread warmer; line the basket with a cloth napkin for wrapping around slices of warm bread. You can even find baskets and bread boards that are tailored for use with long French loaves or round peasant breads.

If your gift recipient is a baker or aspiring baker, substitute bread mixes and baking equipment for fresh loaves. Bread cookbooks and special baking ingredients, such as bread flour or special yeast, are also a nice touch.

PACKAGING Jams & jellies

Homemade jams and jellies are a special gift from the heart and should be presented in a special way. Embellishing the jars that contain them with lid decorations and handmade labels is a simple way to enhance them, and your gift recipient will want to serve your jams and jellies straight from the jar.

These same ideas can be used for purchased specialty preserves, as well. Create a gift collection of regional specialty foods, and decorate the jars with embellishments suggestive of the region. Simply cover up existing labels or carefully soak them off in warm water.

Package your jam or jelly assortment in a gift box surrounded with excelsior, a shredded wood product, or colored tissue. To further accent the gift box, attach dried fruit or dried floral materials to the bow with raffia.

Fabric lid Cover

MATERIALS

❖Jam or jelly of choice ❖Patterned cotton fabric ❖Jute rope ❖Art paper
❖Nail

1 Cut a circle of fabric large enough to fit over the jar lid plus 2" (5 cm) of overhang. Fray the edges by removing several threads from along edges, if desired.

2 Center fabric over lid of jar. Secure with jute around edge of lid.

3 Tear a piece of art paper for the label, and write the jam name on the paper; pierce hole in top corner of the label, using nail.

Paper lid Cover

MATERIALS

❖Jam or jelly of choice ❖Lightweight art paper ❖Aerosol adhesive
❖Narrow gold ribbon

☞ *Seal top of tied ribbon with wax, if desired.*

1 Cut a circle of paper large enough to completely cover top and edge of lid. Apply aerosol adhesive to back of paper. Center paper on lid; press gently to smooth out bubbles, tucking edge of paper just under edge of lid; trim any excess paper.

2 Tie ribbon around jar from bottom to top, securing at top. Tear a second piece of art paper small enough to fit on jar for label. Write jam name on paper. Secure to jar, using aerosol adhesive; press to smooth out air bubbles.

4 Fray ends of jute; knot one end to create tassel. Thread a portion of jute on other end through hole in label; tie end behind label to create tassel.

Cardboard lid Cover

MATERIALS

❖Jam or jelly of choice ❖Raffia ❖Hot glue gun and glue sticks ❖Corrugated cardboard
❖Artificial berry cluster
❖Heavy art paper

1 Wind raffia around edge of the lid several times; secure with hot glue.

2 Cut circle of cardboard large enough to cover lid and extend to edge of raffia. Secure cardboard circle to lid, using hot glue. Secure berry cluster to lid, using hot glue.

3 Tear or cut piece of art paper for label. Write jam name on paper. Secure to the jar, using hot glue.

☞ *Instead of a written label, clip a photo from a seed catalog, to indicate what type of fruit is used for the jam. Secure to jar, using hot glue.*

GIFTS *of* Coffee & tea

Coffee and tea are as popular as ever, and the wide variety of specialty items available is sure to please the coffee and tea drinkers that you know. Assemble a collection of these items in a basket for a simple, yet thoughtful, holiday gift.

Coffee fans will appreciate a pair of mugs accompanied by a selection of gourmet or flavored coffees, and chocolate coffee spoons or chocolate-dipped cinnamon sticks. Small coffee cookbooks are also available for the coffee connoisseur.

If you know a tea-lover, purchase a set of pretty teacups and nestle them in a box or basket with an assortment of teas, a tea ball, tea bag squeezer, tea strainer, honey-filled straws, or flavored tea stirrers that you can make or purchase.

Chocolate coffee Spoons

MATERIALS

❖4 oz. (113 g) high-quality baking or dipping chocolate (sweet dark, semisweet, or white*) ❖1/8 to 1/4 teaspoon (0.5 to 1 mL) oil flavoring of choice, optional ❖2-cup (500 mL) microwaveproof measuring cup ❖15 heavy-duty plastic spoons or decorative flatware spoons ❖Wax paper ❖Baking sheet ❖Plastic wrap ❖Ribbon

*White chocolate is technically not chocolate, but the name is used widely to describe white confection.

1 Break chocolate into small chunks; place chocolate chunks in measuring cup. Microwave at 50% (Medium) for 2 to 3 minutes, or until chocolate is melted, stirring every minute for first 2 minutes, then every 30 seconds. Stir in oil flavoring, if desired.

2 Dip bowl of spoon into chocolate, completely covering bowl. Set the spoon on wax-paper-lined baking sheet. Repeat with the remaining spoons. Allow the spoons to set at room temperature.

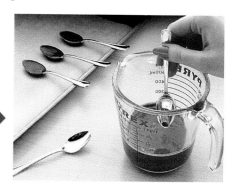

Tea Stirrers

MATERIALS

❖1 cup (250 mL) granulated sugar ❖1/2 cup (125 mL) light corn syrup ❖1/2 cup (125 mL) water ❖1/8 tsp. (0.5 mL) oil flavoring of choice ❖Food coloring of choice ❖2-quart (2 L) saucepan ❖Candy thermometer ❖15 to 20 flatware spoons ❖Baking sheet ❖Nonstick vegetable cooking spray

1 Combine sugar, corn syrup and water in a 1 1/2-qt. (1.5 L) saucepan. Place over high heat, stirring with wooden spoon until mixture comes to a boil. (If sugar crystals are present in saucepan, wash down sides of pan with pastry brush that has been dipped in water.)

3 Wrap bowls of individual spoons with plastic wrap; tie with a ribbon.

☞ *For a cinnamon-chocolate stir stick, dip cinnamon sticks in unflavored chocolate.*

☞ *Oil flavorings are available in some supermarkets, confectioner suppliers, and craft stores.*

☞ *Many chocolates that have been melted have a tendency to "bloom," or get white marks on them, after a few days. For best results, make spoons the day before you plan to give them.*

☞ *Melt chocolate of a different color, and drizzle over bowls of spoon after first chocolate is set. Melted chocolate may also be placed in a squeeze bottle for more controlled drizzling.*

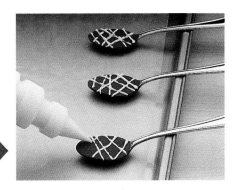

2 Clip the candy thermometer on pan with tip submerged at least 1" (2.5 cm) in the syrup mixture. (Do not let the tip touch the bottom of pan.) Cook syrup, without stirring, to 300°F (150°C) or hard-crack stage, about 5 minutes. Remove from the heat.

☞ *Do not use plastic spoons for this project, since they may melt.*

3 Stir in oil flavoring and food coloring to desired shade. Dip bowl of spoon into syrup, completely covering the bowl, as shown in step 2, opposite. Set spoon on baking sheet that has been sprayed with cooking spray. Repeat with remaining spoons. Allow spoons to set at room temperature.

4 Wrap bowls of individual spoons with plastic wrap; tie with a ribbon.

☞ *For stirring sticks, dip wooden lollipop sticks once or twice into syrup.*

a

b

c

HOMEMADE *Liqueurs*

Liqueurs are a favorite holiday and special-occasion treat, but purchasing name brands for everyone on your gift list can be expensive. Making your own is neither expensive nor time-consuming. Just plan ahead, since homemade liqueurs should stand for one month before serving.

Presenting your special blends can be as much fun as making them. Take advantage of the wide variety of bottles that are available, and embellish them with a small ornament, gift tag, handmade label, or a special bottle stopper. Or wrap the bottle with several layers of colorful tissue gathered at the neck and tied with a ribbon.

Give a bottle in a Christmas stocking surrounded by candy canes; fill the stocking toe with tissue to retain its shape and help lift the bottle out of the stocking. Or nestle a bottle in a box with a set of cordial glasses.

Homemade liqueurs include:

a) Coffee liqueur, *b)* apricot brandy, *c)* anise liqueur, *d)* raspberry liqueur, *e)* crème de menthe.

LIQUEUR RECIPES

Coffee Liqueur

- ❖ 1½ cups (375 mL) sugar
- ❖ 1 cup (250 mL) water
- ❖ ¼ cup (50 mL) instant coffee crystals
- ❖ 1½ cups (375 mL) vodka
- ❖ 1 vanilla bean, split; or 1 teaspoon (5 mL) vanilla extract

Combine sugar and water in 1½-quart (1.5 L) saucepan. Bring to boil over high heat, stirring occasionally. Remove from heat; stir in coffee crystals until dissolved. Cool to room temperature. Skim any foam from top. Stir in remaining ingredients. Pour into bottle; cap. Allow to stand in cool, dark place for 1 month, shaking bottle occasionally to mix.

Makes about 3 cups (750 mL)

Orange Liqueur

- ❖ 3 oranges
- ❖ 1 cup (250 mL) sugar
- ❖ 1 stick cinnamon
- ❖ 2 cups (500 mL) brandy

Remove the peel from one orange with vegetable peeler or zester; do not include white membrane. Cut oranges in half; squeeze out juice—about 1 cup (250 mL). Combine orange peel, juice, sugar, and cinnamon in 1½-quart (1.5 L) saucepan. Bring to boil over high heat; boil 30 seconds. (Watch closely; stir if necessary to prevent boilover.) Remove from heat; cool to room temperature. Strain cooled juice mixture through cheesecloth. Add brandy to the strained liquid. Pour into bottle; cap. Allow to stand in cool, dark place for 1 month, shaking bottle occasionally to mix.

Makes about 3 cups (750 mL)

Crème de Menthe

- ❖ 1½ cups (375 mL) sugar
- ❖ 1 cup (250 mL) water
- ❖ 1½ cups (375 mL) vodka or gin
- ❖ 1 teaspoon (5 mL) peppermint extract
- ❖ ¼ teaspoon (1 mL) green food coloring

Combine sugar and water in 1½-quart (1.5 L) saucepan. Bring to boil over high heat, stirring occasionally. Remove from heat; cool to room temperature. Skim any foam from top. Stir in remaining ingredients. Pour into bottle; cap. Allow to stand in cool, dark place for 1 month, shaking bottle occasionally to mix.

Makes about 4 cups (1 L)

Raspberry Liqueur

- ❖ 2 pkgs. (10 oz./28 g each) frozen raspberries in syrup, defrosted
- ❖ 1½ cups (375 mL) sugar
- ❖ 1½ cups (375 mL) vodka

Strain juice from berries into 2-quart (2 L) saucepan, pressing gently to remove excess juice. Set berries aside. Add sugar to juice. Bring to boil over high heat, stirring frequently until sugar dissolves. Remove from heat; cool to room temperature. Skim any foam from top. Add reserved berries and the vodka. Pour into sealable container; seal. Allow to stand in cool, dark place for 1 month, shaking occasionally to mix. Strain mixture through cheesecloth; discard solids. Pour liqueur into bottle; cap.

Makes 3 cups (750 mL)

Apricot Brandy

- ❖ 1 pkg. (6 oz./170 g) dried apricots, chopped
- ❖ 1½ cups (375 mL) white wine
- ❖ 1 cup (250 mL) sugar
- ❖ 1 cup (250 mL) brandy

Combine apricots, wine, and sugar in 1½-quart (1.5 L) saucepan. Bring to boil over high heat, stirring frequently until sugar dissolves. Remove from heat; cool to room temperature. Skim any foam from top. Stir in brandy. Pour into sealable container; seal. Allow to stand in cool, dark place for 1 month, shaking occasionally to mix. Strain mixture through cheesecloth; discard solids. Pour liqueur into bottle; cap.

Makes about 2 cups (500 mL)

Anise Liqueur

- ❖ 1½ cups (375 mL) light corn syrup
- ❖ ½ cup (125 mL) water
- ❖ ¼ teaspoon (1 mL) instant unflavored, unsweetened tea powder
- ❖ 1½ cups (375 mL) vodka
- ❖ ¾ teaspoon (4 mL) anise extract
- ❖ ½ teaspoon (2 mL) vanilla
- ❖ 2 drops yellow food coloring

Combine corn syrup, water, and tea powder in 1½-quart (1.5 L) saucepan. Bring to boil over high heat. Remove from heat; cool to room temperature. Skim any foam from top. Stir in remaining ingredients. Pour into bottle; cap. Allow to stand in cool dark place for 1 month, shaking bottle occasionally to mix.

Makes about 4 cups (1 L)

61

METAL
Ornaments

The holidays evoke images of sparkling lights and warm glows. Ornaments made of metal cheerfully reflect those holiday lights. Copper not only casts a warming shimmer, but can be further enhanced by heat oxidation or given a verdigris finish with a patina solution.

Create your own handcrafted ornaments by cutting and treating sheets of copper or tin, which are available in craft stores. Or simply purchase any of a wide variety of cookie cutters, embellish them, and punch holes in them for hangers. Make individual ornaments or string them together with ribbon, raffia, or wire to create a garland. Embellish garland with beads and other adornments, if desired.

Copper or tin Ornaments

MATERIALS

❖Copper or tin sheet ❖Cookie cutters
❖Awl and rubber mallet, or tin-punching tool ❖Scrap of wood ❖Utility scissors
❖100-grit sandpaper ❖Fine steel wool
❖Aerosol clear acrylic sealer
❖Ribbon, raffia, or
wire for hanger

1 Trace design on metal sheet with a pencil, using a cookie cutter as a template. Place design over scrap of wood. Punch hole for hanger about 1/8" (3 mm) inside top edge of design, using awl and mallet. Embellish interior of ornament with a punched design, shown below, if desired.

Punched Design

MATERIALS

❖Metal ornament ❖Awl ❖Rubber mallet or hammer

1 Tape a design drawn on paper to metal sheet inside lines for ornament. Punch holes around the edges of design at 1/8" (3 mm) intervals, using awl and mallet. Remove paper. Continue as in steps 2 and 3, above.

2 Cut out ornament with scissors. Trim the tips off any sharp points; slightly round points, if desired. Lightly sand the edges of ornament with sandpaper to smooth any sharp edges; avoid sanding surface of ornament if smooth finish is desired. If a textured finish is desired, rub surface lightly with sandpaper.

3 Rub ornament lightly with fine steel wool to remove any fingerprints. Wipe clean. If desired, oxidize (below) or use patina solution as in tip, below, on copper. Spray ornament with acrylic sealer. Thread ribbon, raffia, or wire through hole at top of ornament for hanger.

☞ *Trace several designs on single sheet of metal before cutting.*

☞ *If a verdigris finish is desired, apply a patina solution, such as Modern Options' Patina Green™, following manufacturer's directions.*

☞ *If sharp edges are raised on back of ornament after punching with awl, lightly hammer edges flat with rubber mallet.*

1 Sand the surface of copper ornament lightly with sandpaper. Using tongs, hold the ornament over a flame, such as a gas stove burner. Move ornament randomly through the flame to produce color change, removing from the heat occasionally to check for the desired color. Continue as in step 3, above.

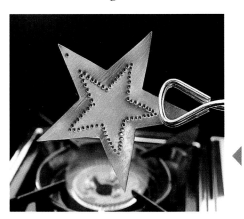

Oxidized Copper

MATERIALS

❖Copper ornament ❖Long tongs with insulated handles

☞ *Holding copper in flame too long can cause it to lose all its natural color.*

Papier-mâché
ORNAMENTS

Create easy-to-make papier-mâché ornaments from ready-made forms, available at craft stores. Simply embellish the forms with a variety of paints, beads, or glitter for shimmering holiday gifts.

Paint ornaments with aerosol acrylic paint—use a pearlescent paint for a lustrous finish. Apply glitter glue to painted ornaments to create a shining raised design. Embellish painted ornaments with beads, ribbons, and cording secured in place with craft glue.

Woodland ORNAMENTS

Making your own unique woodland ornaments takes very little time and few materials. You could check off everyone on your gift list with just one trip to the craft store and one afternoon's work.

Make several different ornaments, using similar materials, or make a set of identical ornaments, and package them together in a nice gift box. Having several ornaments with similar elements gives unity and a theme to any Christmas tree.

Pinecone Ornament

MATERIALS

❖Two pinecones ❖Hot glue gun and glue sticks ❖Artificial berry clusters ❖Dried leaves and sprigs of eucalyptus ❖Sheet moss or Spanish moss, optional ❖Raffia or ribbon, for hanger

1 Attach pinecones side by side at their base end, using hot glue. Hold pinecones together until glue has set.

2 Secure two berry clusters to base end of pinecones, using hot glue, so one cluster cascades toward tips of pinecones on each side. Glue a few dried leaves and sprigs of the eucalyptus between berry stems.

3 Tie raffia or ribbon into a loop; tuck knotted end into base of the arrangement, and secure with hot glue.

4 Fill in gaps and cover the stems of berries and leaves with additional leaves or moss; secure with hot glue.

☞ *If desired, paint pinecones gold with aerosol acrylic paint before beginning project.*

Miniature Wreath

MATERIALS

❖Miniature grapevine wreath ❖Preserved cedar and artificial pine sprigs ❖Hot glue gun and glue sticks ❖Artificial berries ❖Small craft bird ❖Jute or raffia, for hanger

1 Secure cedar and pine sprigs to bottom of wreath, using hot glue. Embellish wreath with berries.

2 Secure bird inside wreath so it sits on pine branches, using hot glue. Tie jute or raffia around the top of wreath, and form loop for hanger.

1 Secure cinnamon sticks together one at a time at their centers to create a small bundle. Secure the holly sprig to center of bundle, using hot glue.

2 Tie ribbon around center of bundle to conceal any hot glue drops. Tie loop at center of ornament for hanger.

Cinnamon-stick Bundle

MATERIALS

❖Several long cinnamon sticks ❖Artificial holly sprig ❖Ribbon or raffia, for hanger ❖Hot glue gun and glue sticks

☞ *To save money, purchase cinnamon sticks in bulk at food co-ops or craft stores.*

1 Wrap pine garland around base of cone; secure with hot glue. Embellish garland with berries.

2 Secure bird to top of leaf. Secure leaf to pinecone just above garland.

Single Pinecone

MATERIALS

❖Pinecone ❖Artificial pine garland and berries ❖Hot glue gun and glue sticks ❖Small craft bird ❖Artificial leaf ❖Raffia or ribbon, for hanger

3 Tie raffia or ribbon around tip of pinecone; then tie in loop for hanger.

Woven village GIFTS

Collectible holiday villages are favorite gifts for many people to give and receive. Create your own series of woven village wall ornaments to give to the collectors on your gift list.

You can design a different style every year and add an embellishment that shows the year it was made. Or try to pattern your woven houses after the homes of your gift recipients.

Weave your village from strips of birch bark, corrugated art paper, handmade papers, or even heavy fabrics. Accent them with twigs, pieces of rope, paper twist, greenery, or other embellishments. You might even add tiny flower boxes under the windows.

Woven village Gifts

MATERIALS

❖Weaving material, such as birch bark, corrugated art paper, handmade paper, heavy fabric ❖Cardboard box ❖Thumb tacks ❖Mat knife and cutting mat, or craft scissors ❖Trim material, such as paper twist, sisal rope, twigs, cording ❖Embellishments ❖Awl ❖Narrow ribbon or raffia

1 Draw the outline of your house design on plain paper. Measure the height and width of the pattern to determine the

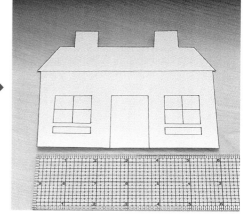

length and number of ½" (1.3 cm) strips of weaving material you will need. Add 1" to 2" (2.5 to 5 cm) of length to each strip. For example, if your house is to be 5" (12.5 cm) high and 6" (15 cm) wide, you will need at least 12 vertical strips that are 6" to 7" (15 to 18 cm) long. The number of horizontal strips will depend on how tight a weave you want.

2 Cut strips from weaving material, using mat knife or craft scissors. On inverted cardboard box or a piece of thick cardboard, secure vertical strips side by side on one end with thumb tacks.

3 Weave horizontal strips through vertical strips, alternating rows with each new strip. The finished woven piece will be larger than your pattern.

▶

4 Cut trim material to match outline of house pattern. Lightly sketch outline on woven piece with pencil. Secure pieces of trim material along pencil outline, using hot glue.

5 Secure pieces of trim material to house for door and windows, using hot glue. Embellish house as desired. At top center of house, make a hole with awl.

6 Remove house from cardboard box. Trim excess weaving strips from around the edge of house, using mat knife or craft scissors. Thread ribbon or raffia through hole in top center of house, and tie a loop for a hanger.

▶

75

SCENTED GIFTS:
Potpourri

Potpourri makes a decorative room accent that emits delicate aromas. Presented in a pretty bowl, it makes an ideal gift. You can create your own potpourri blends with the fragrance, look, and colors you desire.

Essential oils are combined with dried naturals to create potpourri. The oils enhance the scents of the plant materials while adding fragrance of their own. Essential oils are available in craft stores, beauty salons, health food stores, and bath shops. They range in scent from sweet to spicy to woodsy.

Fixatives are necessary to absorb and retain the scents of your potpourri. Orris root, calamus, and cellulose-fiber fixatives are available in craft stores and from mail-order suppliers. Some spices, such as cumin seeds, coriander, cloves, nutmeg, and cinnamon, act as fixatives, as do broken corn cobs, frankincense, cedarwood, gum benzoin, oak moss, and oil of sandalwood. In potpourri, more than one type of fixative is often used.

Wildflower Blend

- ❖ 1 oz. (25 g) orris root powder or 1/4 cup (50 mL) cut orris root, chopped calamus, or cellulose-fiber fixative
- ❖ Four drops geranium essential oil
- ❖ Three drops lavender essential oil
- ❖ 1 qt. (1 L) mixed dried flower petals and heads
- ❖ 1 cup (250 mL) dried globe amaranth blossoms
- ❖ 4 oz. (125 g) lavender
- ❖ 2 oz. (50 g) lemon verbena leaves
- ❖ 1 oz. (25 g) uva ursi or oregano leaves
- ❖ 10 to 12 cinnamon sticks, 3" (7.5 cm) long
- ❖ Small dried sunflower blossoms, for embellishment

Rose Blend

- ❖ 1 oz. (25 g) orris root powder or 1/4 cup (50 mL) cut orris root, chopped calamus, or cellulose-fiber fixative
- ❖ 1/2 teaspoon (2 mL) ground cinnamon
- ❖ Four drops rose essential oil
- ❖ 1 qt. (1 L) dried mixed rose petals
- ❖ 1 cup (250 mL) dried globe amaranth blossoms
- ❖ 2 oz. (50 g) lavender
- ❖ 5 or 6 star anise
- ❖ 1/2 teaspoon (2 mL) whole cloves
- ❖ A few dried rose leaves, for color
- ❖ Additional dried rose heads and leaves, for embellishment

Making Potpourri

🎁

1 Place fixative and any ground spices in bowl; add drops of essential oils. Mix thoroughly.

Citrus Blend

- ❖ 1 oz. (25 g) orris root powder or 1/4 cup (50 mL) cut orris root, chopped calamus, or cellulose-fiber fixative
- ❖ 1 1/2 teaspoons (7 mL) ground nutmeg
- ❖ Four drops citrus essential oil
- ❖ Two drops frankincense essential oil
- ❖ 1 qt. (1 L) dried orange, lemon, or lime slices
- ❖ 4 oz. (125 g) dried lemon peel
- ❖ 2 oz. (50 g) eucalyptus leaves
- ❖ 1 oz. (25 g) each of tilia and kesu flowers
- ❖ 10 to 12 each of bay leaves and star anise
- ❖ 10 to 12 cinnamon sticks, 3" (7.5 cm) long
- ❖ 1 tablespoon (15 mL) juniper berries
- ❖ Small dried sunflower blossoms, for embellishment

Pine-forest Blend

- ❖ 1 oz. (25 g) orris root powder or 1/4 cup (50 mL) cut orris root, chopped calamus, or cellulose-fiber fixative
- ❖ Four drops pine essential oil
- ❖ Two drops eucalyptus essential oil
- ❖ Two drops sandalwood essential oil
- ❖ 1 qt. (1 L) mixture of small pinecones, slivered birch bark, green eucalyptus, and princess pine and cedar needles
- ❖ 10 to 15 poppy pods
- ❖ 10 to 12 cinnamon sticks, 3" (7.5 cm) long
- ❖ 1/2 oz. (15 g) curly pods
- ❖ 1/2 teaspoon (2 mL) whole cloves
- ❖ Large pinecones, for embellishment

2 Add remaining ingredients, except embellishments, to bowl. Mix thoroughly to evenly distribute ingredients.

3 Place potpourri in airtight container. Store potpourri and embellishments in dry, dark place for at least six weeks; shake potpourri container daily for first week. The longer potpourri is stored, the more its fragrance matures.

4 Place the potpourri in decorative open container. Embellish with reserved naturals. Store unused potpourri in an airtight container.

DECORATED
Table linens

Tablecloths, placemats, table runners, and napkins can be easily decorated with holiday designs and given as gifts. Purchase those with simple styles and colors, and embellish them in a variety of ways.

Stitch fabric trims, fusible appliqués, and tassels onto linens. Trace designs from stencils, adapt artwork from greeting cards, or create original designs and then paint table linens. Secure decorative jewels and nail heads to linens with fabric glue. Or decorate heavy craft paper or cardboard to make disposable table coverings for children or large groups.

Jewel-studded Linens

MATERIALS

❖Purchased tablecloth, placemats, table runner, or napkins ❖Decorative imitation jewels, nail heads, or buttons ❖Fabric glue or jewelry glue

1 Embellish table linens as desired with decorative jewels, nail heads, or buttons. Secure nail heads by piercing fabric with pointed backs; bend points on back of the linen. Secure jewels and buttons with glue. ▶

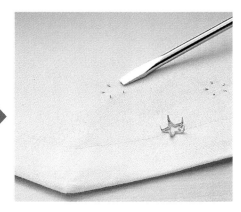

Painted table Linens

MATERIALS

❖Purchased tablecloth, placemats, table runner, or napkins ❖Textile paints, including metallic paints, if desired ❖Artist's brushes and stencil brush ❖Pictorial design book or stencils, if desired ❖Masking tape, pressure-sensitive tape, or painter's tape

☞ *Practice painting techniques on fabric scraps or paper before painting linens.*

STENCILED DESIGNS

Position stencils as desired on linens; secure, using masking tape. Apply paint within cut areas of stencil, using up-and-down motion with brush. ▼

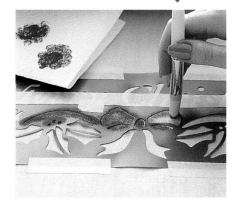

1 Cut cardboard or craft paper to the desired size for placemats. Draw or paint holiday designs on placemats.

☞ *For a children's table, provide the children with blank placemats and crayons, paints, or markers before the meal. Allow them to decorate their own.*

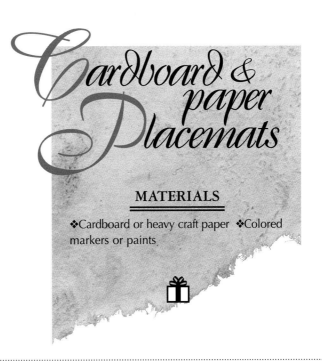

Cardboard & paper Placemats

MATERIALS

❖Cardboard or heavy craft paper ❖Colored markers or paints

GEOMETRIC DESIGNS

Use artwork in pictorial books for geometric design ideas. Mark lines on fabric, using pencil and straightedge. Apply painter's tape and pressure-sensitive tape alongside designs before applying paint, for clean edges.

SPATTERED DESIGNS

Dilute paint that will be used for spattered effect. Wet brush with paint, and tap the brush to spatter the paint onto linens.

WOOLEN *M*antel stockings

Turn woolen socks, available at stores specializing in outdoor clothing, into one-of-a-kind Christmas stockings. Fill them with small gifts, candy, fruit, or nuts before giving them away.

Choose trims and embellishments that complement the homespun look of the stockings. Add patches of flannel or wool fabric and trims, such as bells, buttons, appliqués, or fringe. Turn down the top of the sock for a cuff.

Most items can be stitched in place, using a darning needle and narrow ribbon, yarn, or pearl cotton. Insert a cardboard liner, cut slightly larger than the sock, into the stocking when stitching to avoid catching stitches in the back of the stocking. Knot a loop of ribbon through the top of the sock, for a hanger.

MINIATURE *Floral* arrangements

Miniature floral arrangements are thoughtful, decorative gifts for brightening spots like windowsills, desks, shelves, or countertops. Make arrangements in holiday colors, or customize them to match the colors in someone's home.

Miniature baskets and clay or wooden pots are available at craft stores. Since very few materials are necessary for each arrangement, you can stretch materials to make several styles with a similar look. If desired, add ribbon loops to the arrangements so they can be used as tree ornaments.

Flower Basket

MATERIALS

❖Miniature basket ❖Floral foam ❖Hot glue gun and glue sticks ❖Sheet moss or Spanish moss ❖Dried and preserved naturals, cut into 2" (5 cm) lengths ❖Artificial berries ❖Small craft bird

1 Cut a piece of floral foam to fit in the basket. Secure foam in bottom of basket, using hot glue. Cover the foam with moss; secure with hot glue, if necessary.

2 Insert several evenly spaced sprigs of dried and preserved naturals into foam. Fill spaces between naturals with berries; secure, using hot glue. Secure bird to edge of basket, using hot glue.

☞ *Select dried naturals to suit the season.*

1 Cut a piece of floral foam to fit in pot. Secure the foam in bottom of pot, using hot glue. (If desired, place a rock, for weight, in bottom of pot, under foam, for stability.)

2 Insert three or four twigs in center of foam to form the "trunk" of topiary. Secure, using hot glue at base of trunk.

3 Secure small piece of pine around trunk base to conceal foam. Wind a few pieces of pine into ball. Secure ball to top of twigs, using hot glue. Accent ball of pine with berries; secure, using hot glue.

Miniature Topiary

MATERIALS

❖Miniature wooden pot ❖Floral foam
❖Hot glue gun and glue sticks ❖Twigs, cut to equal lengths ❖Artificial pine garland ❖Artificial berries

☞ *Embellish topiary with narrow gold cording wrapped around trunk, if desired.*

☞ *Paint wooden pot with acrylic craft paint, if desired.*

1 Cut a piece of floral foam to fit in pot. Secure foam in bottom of pot, using hot glue.

2 Insert berries, leaves, and naturals into foam for desired appearance; trim stems as necessary to fit pot. If necessary, secure embellishments in pot, using hot glue.

Terra-cotta pot Arrangement

MATERIALS

❖Small terra-cotta pot ❖Floral foam
❖Hot glue gun and glue sticks
❖Artificial berries and leaves ❖Dried or artificial naturals

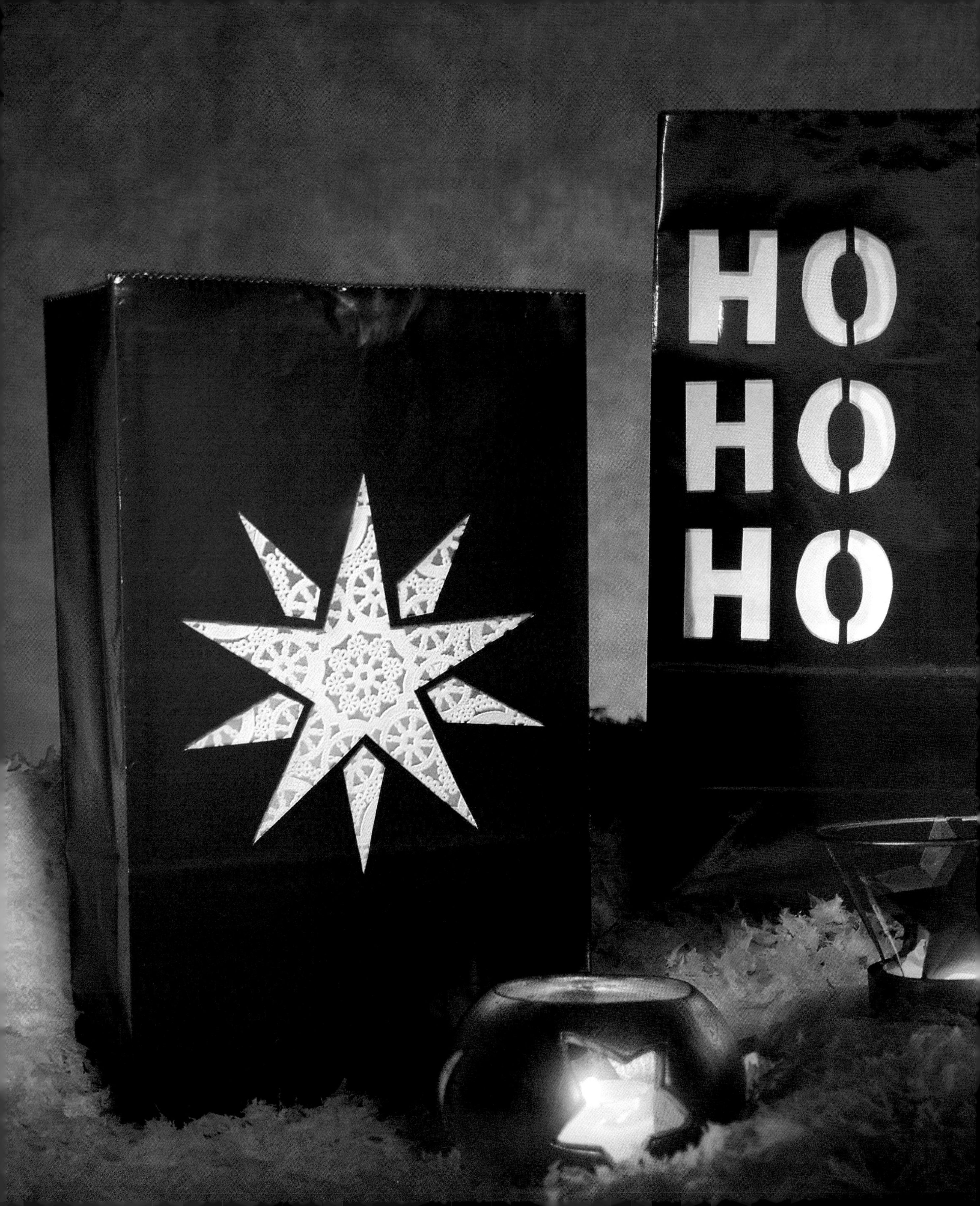
HO
HO
HO

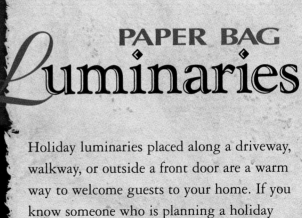

PAPER BAG
Luminaries

Holiday luminaries placed along a driveway, walkway, or outside a front door are a warm way to welcome guests to your home. If you know someone who is planning a holiday party, delight them with an assortment of these simple, festive lights.

By placing a light-colored bag inside a dark-colored bag with a holiday motif cutout, you can create a wide variety of patterned luminaries. Make several luminaries with the same design or mix up the designs and the colors. You can even dress up your luminaries with lace doilies.

Paper bag Luminaries

MATERIALS

❖ Mat board or piece of heavy cardboard; mat knife ❖ Dark-colored paper bags ❖ Cookie cutters or stencils ❖ Light-colored paper bags ❖ Sand ❖ Votive candles

1 Cut piece of mat board or cardboard so it will fit inside paper bag. The board will protect your work surface and prevent you from cutting through both sides of the bag.

2 Trace designs or words on the dark bag using cookie cutters or stencils as templates; trace with a pencil.

3 Insert mat board or cardboard into bag; cut designs out of bags with mat knife.

▶

4 Remove mat board from bag. Insert light bag into dark bag, and unfold. Fill bottom of layered bags with sand; nestle candle in sand in bottom of bag.

☞ *For easier packaging, fold up bags, and give sand and votive candles in separate bags with instructions on assembly.*

☞ *If desired, cut a paper doily slightly larger than the cutout design on dark bag. (Edges should not be ragged, because their silhouette may show through bag.) Secure doily to inside of dark bag so that it is centered, using glue stick.*

▶

☞ *For a confetti-like look, use colored markers to make spots on light bag. Cut out holes in dark bag to reveal spots.*

INDEX

☙ CREDITS

CY DECOSSE INCORPORATED

Chairman/CEO: Bruce Barnet
Chairman Emeritus: Cy DeCosse
President/COO: Nino Tarantino
Executive V.P./Editor-in-Chief:
  William B. Jones

GREET THE SEASON
Created by: The Editors of
  Cy DeCosse Incorporated

Also available from the publisher:
*Grand Slam Gifts, Toast the Host,
Wrap It Up*

Group Executive Editor: Zoe A. Graul
Editorial Manager: Dawn M. Anderson
Senior Editor/Writer: Ellen C. Boeke
Project Manager: Amy Berndt
Associate Creative Director: Lisa Rosenthal
Art Director: Stephanie Michaud
Editor: Janice Cauley

Researcher/Designer: Michael Basler
Sample Production Manager: Carol Olson
Technical Photo Stylists: Bridget Haugh,
  Sue Jorgensen, Nancy Sundeen
Styling Director: Bobbette Destiche
Project Stylists: Christine Jahns,
  Joanne Wawra
Prop Stylist: Michelle Joy
Food Stylists: Elizabeth Emmons,
  Nancy Johnson
Artisans: Arlene Dohrman,
  Phyllis Galbraith, Kristi Kuhnau,
  Virginia Mateen, Carol Pilot,
  Michelle Skudlarek
*Vice President of Development Planning &
  Production:* Jim Bindas
Director of Photography: Mike Parker
Creative Photo Coordinator:
  Cathleen Shannon
Studio Manager: Marcia Chambers
Lead Photographer: Mark Macemon
Photographers: Rex Irmen, Charles Nields,
  Mike Parker, Rebecca Schmitt
Contributing Photographers: Paul Najlis,
  Steve Smith
Print Production Manager: Patt Sizer
Desktop Publishing Specialist:
  Laurie Kristensen
Production Staff: Laura Hokkanen,
  Tom Hoops, Jeanette Moss, Mike Schauer,

Michael Sipe, Brent Thomas, Greg Wallace,
  Kay Wethern
Shop Supervisor: Phil Juntti
Scenic Carpenters: Troy Johnson,
  Rob Johnstone, John Nadeau
Contributors: Cookies by Design; Design
  Master; Duff Associates; Forestsaver; Honey
  Wax; Plaid Enterprises; Tolin' Station
Sources for Product Information:
  Beeswax candle sheets—Honey Wax,
  P.O. Box 370, Hackensack, MN 56452,
  (800) 880-7694

  Oil flavoring; baking and dipping
  chocolate—Sweet Celebrations,
  P.O. Box 39426, Edina, MN 55439,
  (800) 328-6722
Printed on American paper by:
  R. R. Donnelley & Sons Co. (0796)
99 98 97 96 / 5 4 3 2 1

Cy DeCosse Incorporated offers
a variety of how-to books. For
information write:
  Cy DeCosse Subscriber Books
  5900 Green Oak Drive
  Minnetonka, MN 55343